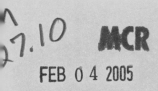

DATE DUE

NOV 1 2 2005	

DEMCO, INC. 38-2931

Scientists at Work

Astronomers

Julie Haydon

Smart Apple Media

This edition first published in 2005 in the United States of America by Smart Apple Media.

Smart Apple Media
1980 Lookout Drive
North Mankato
Minnesota 56003

Library of Congress Cataloging-in-Publication Data

Haydon, Julie.
   Astronomers / by Julie Haydon.
   p. cm. — (Scientists at work)
   Includes index.
   ISBN 1-58340-541-0 (alk. paper)
   1. Astronomy—Vocational guidance.—Juvenile literature. 2. Astronomers—Juvenile
literature. [1. Astronomers. 2. Astronomy—Vocational guidance. 3. Vocational guidance.]
   I. Title. II. Scientists at work (Smart Apple Media)

   QB51.5.H39 2004
   520'.92—dc22   2003070429

First Edition
9 8 7 6 5 4 3 2 1

First published in 2004 by
MACMILLAN EDUCATION AUSTRALIA PTY LTD
627 Chapel Street, South Yarra, Australia, 3141

Associated companies and representatives throughout the world.

Edited by Sally Woollett
Text and cover design by The Modern Art Production Group
Page layout by Raul Diche
Photo research by Jesmondene Senbergs
Printed in China

Acknowledgements
The author and the publisher are grateful to the following for permission to reproduce copyright material:
Cover photograph: Astronomers using a telescope, courtesy of Corbis.

© Anglo-Australian Observatory, pp. 14 (top left), 18; Astrovisuals, p. 14 (top right); Reg Morrison/
Auscape, p. 28 (bottom); Corbis, pp. 4, 6, 12, 17, 19, 20; Digital Vision, pp. 11, 25; Getty Images, p. 21;
Mary Evans Picture Library, pp. 7, 8, 10; Melbourne Planetarium, p. 30; NASA, pp. 14 (bottom right), 15
(top left, bottom left), 26; NASA Ames Research Center, p. 22; NASA/L-3 Communications Integrated
Systems, p. 23; Photodisc, pp. 14 (bottom left), 15 (top right, bottom right), 27, 28 (top); Photo Essentials,
p. 16; Photolibrary.com/SPL, p. 13; Science Photo Library, p. 5; NASA/Science Photo Library, p. 9; © The
Picture Source/Terry Oakley, p. 29 (all).

Author acknowledgements
Many thanks to Dr. Yvonne Pendleton, for kindly agreeing to be interviewed for this book. Thanks also to
Dr. Tanya Hill and Dr. John O'Byrne for their reviews of the first draft, and to Susana Deustua of the
American Astronomical Society.

While every care has been taken to trace and acknowledge copyright, the publisher tenders their
apologies for any accidental infringement where copyright has proved untraceable. Where the attempt has
been unsuccessful, the publisher welcomes information that would redress the situation.

Please note
At the time of printing, the Internet addresses appearing in this book were correct. Owing to the dynamic nature of the Internet, however, we cannot guarantee that all these addresses will remain correct.

Contents

Glossary words

When you see a word printed in **bold**, you can look up its meaning in the glossary on page 31.

What is an astronomer?

An astronomer is a scientist who studies the universe. The universe is huge. It contains galaxies, planets, stars, moons, and many other **celestial** objects, including the Earth, sun, and moon. It also contains gas and dust.

The universe is so big that most astronomers specialize, which means they focus their studies in one area. An astronomer might study our solar system, our galaxy, distant galaxies, planets, the stars, or the sun. Some astronomers study the universe as a whole. They want to understand how everything in the universe came to be, and how it all fits together.

Scientists
working together

Astronomers often work with other scientists, such as physicists. Physicists study the physical world and how it works. Many astronomers are called astrophysicists. Astronomers sometimes study the data that other physicists have collected and use it to try to work out what is happening in space.

Astronomers use many different instruments to study the universe. Observational astronomers use instruments such as large, powerful telescopes to get images and make measurements of celestial objects. This scientific information, called data, may also come from equipment aboard spacecraft. Theoretical astronomers work mainly on computers to **simulate** astronomical events, and to develop and test scientific **theories** about space.

Observational astronomers use instruments such as telescopes to study the universe.

4

The role of astronomers

Astronomers play an important role in our world. They help us to understand the Earth's place in space and they help us learn about celestial objects. They search for the answers to questions about the origin of the universe, its workings, and its future.

Everything that exists, all **matter** and energy, makes up the universe. Astronomers want to understand how and when all matter and energy began. They also want to know where it is, what it is made of, how much there is, and how it all behaves and changes. Astronomers also want to know if the universe will end, and if life exists anywhere other than Earth.

Thanks to the work of astronomers, we now understand why we have day and night, seasons, **phases** of the moon, and eclipses. We know how the sun makes heat and light. We know what nearby planets look like. We know there are solar systems and galaxies beyond our own, and that there are amazing objects in space, such as **black holes**.

Everything that exists makes up the universe.

Astronomy in the past

In early times, people looked up at the sky and wondered about the stars, sun, and moon. Although they did not know what these objects were, they recognized cycles. The sun appeared to rise each morning and move across the sky, before it set each night. The moon moved and appeared to change shape regularly. The stars appeared to travel across the sky in fixed groups. Different seasons came and went. These events affected hunting, sleeping, and traveling.

This is the constellation Orion.

Astronomy in daily life

Over time, people created calendars based on celestial cycles so they would know when to plant and harvest crops. They also made simple clocks and compasses. Religious and social ceremonies were often tied to celestial events.

People created songs, stories, and paintings to celebrate the beauty, power, and mystery of objects in the sky. They saw patterns, called constellations, in the stars, and gave these patterns names such as Orion the Hunter.

Key events in astronomy

B.C.
Prehistoric humans wonder about celestial objects, and notice cycles.

200s B.C.
Aristarchus of Samos proposes that the Earth turns on its axis once a day and revolves around the sun.

1543
Copernicus writes that the sun is the center of the universe.

1600s
Johannes Kepler develops three laws based on the movements of planets.

350 B.C.
Aristotle argues the Earth is round because it casts a curved shadow on the moon during a lunar eclipse.

A.D. 140
Ptolemy writes that the Earth is the center of the universe.

1609–1610
Galileo uses a telescope to study the sky. He sees that Venus has phases, and that moons orbit Jupiter.

Progress in astronomy

Over 2,000 years ago, most people believed that the Earth was flat, and that it was the center of the universe.

Copernicus wrote that the planets move around the sun. Few people believed him.

The Earth is round

In 350 B.C., a Greek scientist named Aristotle (384–322 B.C.) argued that the Earth is round because the shadow cast on the moon by the Earth during a **lunar eclipse** is curved. He also noted that when a person travels north or south, different stars are visible in the sky.

The Earth orbits the sun

Around A.D. 140, Ptolemy (about A.D. 100–170), an astronomer in Egypt, wrote a book describing the movements of the sun, moon, stars, and planets around the Earth. Ptolemy's ideas, though wrong, were accepted for centuries.

In 1543, a Polish astronomer, Copernicus (1473–1543), published a book stating that the planets, including the Earth, move around the sun. Few people believed him. In the early 1600s, an Italian astronomer, Galileo (1564–1642), used the newly invented telescope to look at the sky. He noticed, amongst other things, that Venus has phases, just like the moon. This means Venus moves around the sun. Galileo believed Copernicus was right. The Earth is not the center of the universe. The planets move around the sun.

Other important discoveries about the universe were to come. These would completely change astronomy.

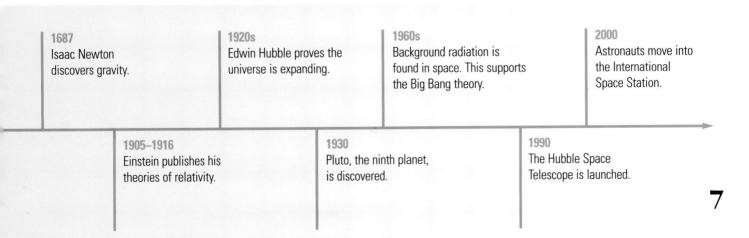

1687
Isaac Newton discovers gravity.

1920s
Edwin Hubble proves the universe is expanding.

1960s
Background radiation is found in space. This supports the Big Bang theory.

2000
Astronauts move into the International Space Station.

1905–1916
Einstein publishes his theories of relativity.

1930
Pluto, the ninth planet, is discovered.

1990
The Hubble Space Telescope is launched.

Important discoveries

Many important discoveries have helped astronomers learn more about the universe.

The movements of planets

In the early 1600s, Johannes Kepler (1571–1630), a German astronomer, developed three laws based on the movements of planets. The first law is that the orbit of a planet around the sun is not a circle, but an oval shape called an ellipse. The second law is that the closer a planet gets to the sun, the faster it moves. The third law is that the time a planet takes to orbit the sun relates to its distance from the sun. Kepler's laws were an important step in understanding how planets move. However, Kepler did not know why planets orbit the Sun.

Isaac Newton discovered the universal force known as gravity.

Gravity

In 1687, British scientist Isaac Newton (1642–1727) described a universal force known as gravity. Gravity is the force of attraction between any object and any other object. When an apple falls from a tree, gravity (the force of attraction between the apple and the Earth) pulls it towards the Earth. The moon orbits the Earth because of the Earth's gravitational pull. The planets orbit the sun because of the sun's gravitational pull.

8

Other galaxies

Early last century, many astronomers believed our galaxy, the Milky Way, was the only galaxy. Then in the 1920s, Edwin Hubble, an American astronomer, proved that there are galaxies beyond our own. Hubble also proved that the universe is not still, but is in fact expanding (getting larger). He found that the farther away a galaxy is, the faster it is moving away from us. This is known as Hubble's law.

The Big Bang

Astronomers are not certain how the universe began, but most believe it was formed in a massive explosion billions of years ago called the Big Bang. Matter was created in the explosion, and very slowly became celestial objects such as galaxies, stars, and planets. Time, space, and energy were also created by the Big Bang. Since the Big Bang, the universe has been expanding and cooling.

In the 1960s, two physicists, Arno Penzias and Robert Wilson, working in the United States, found evidence to support the Big Bang theory. With a radio telescope, they detected a weak glow (**microwave radiation**) in space. The glow would not go away, and was coming from all over the universe. Astronomers think this background radiation is the cooling remains of energy from the Big Bang.

In 1989, the National Aeronautics and Space Administration (NASA), an American government agency, launched the Cosmic Background Explorer (COBE) satellite to measure and map background radiation. Then, in 2001, NASA launched the Wilkinson Microwave Anisotropy Probe (WMAP) to get more detailed data. The data obtained by COBE and WMAP supports the Big Bang theory.

The COBE satellite measured and mapped light left over from the Big Bang.

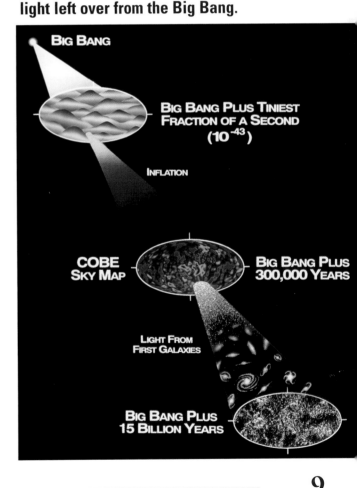

BIG BANG

BIG BANG PLUS TINIEST FRACTION OF A SECOND (10^{-43})

INFLATION

COBE SKY MAP

BIG BANG PLUS 300,000 YEARS

LIGHT FROM FIRST GALAXIES

BIG BANG PLUS 15 BILLION YEARS

Famous astronomer

Who is the famous astronomer described below? Read the notes and work it out!

Who am I?

My early and middle years

I was born in 1564 in Pisa, Italy.

I began studying medicine at the University of Pisa in 1581, but I did not finish my degree.

I was fascinated by mathematics, so I studied privately under a famous mathematician.

In 1589, I began teaching mathematics at the University of Pisa. Later I taught at the University of Padua, Italy.

In 1609, I heard of a spyglass (a telescope) from Holland (the Netherlands) that could make distant objects seem closer. Without seeing a spyglass, I made my own.

In 1609, I looked at the night sky through one of my telescopes. I saw that the surface of the moon was uneven and rough. It even had mountains and craters. This did not match the common view that celestial bodies were perfect, smooth spheres.

In early 1610, I saw moons around Jupiter through my telescope. I watched the moons over several weeks and saw that they orbit the planet. I realized Copernicus was right when he wrote that the Earth is not the center of the universe.

I published my findings in a book called "The Starry Messenger."

"I made my own telescope and studied the night sky."

My later years

In late 1610, I watched Venus go through phases, in the same way as the moon. I knew I was seeing the light of the sun reflecting off the planet as Venus orbited the sun. I believed this proved Copernicus' theory that the Earth moves around the sun.

In 1613, I published a book that discussed **sunspots**. The existence of sunspots means the sun is not a perfect, unchanging sphere. My belief that the Earth moves around the sun also became known. This angered many people who thought I was speaking against what was written in the Bible.

In 1616, the Catholic Church ordered me not to hold or defend the view that the Earth moves.

In 1632, I published a book called "Dialogue Concerning the Two Chief World Systems." (Before it was published, the Church checked the manuscript and wrote the beginning and end.)

In 1633, I was put on trial by the Church for suspicion of **heresy**. I was condemned to life imprisonment and forced to **abjure**. My book "Dialogue" was banned.

I was kept a prisoner under house arrest in various comfortable homes before I was allowed to move to my villa near Florence, where I spent the rest of my life.

I went blind in 1637.

In 1638, I published my last book, "Discourses Concerning Two New Sciences."

I died in 1642.

My initials are G.G.

I am ...

Fact Box

In 1992, the Catholic Church formally acknowledged it made an error of judgement where this astronomer was concerned.

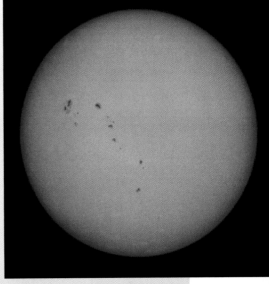

"The existence of sunspots means the sun is not a perfect, unchanging sphere."

Hint: Try searching the Internet to find the answer. (See page 32 for the answer.)

Training to be an astronomer

Astronomers work in a number of different fields, but they all need to learn certain common skills. Astronomers become qualified by studying at college.

At school

Astronomy is a science, so high school students who want to become astronomers need to study subjects such as math, physics, chemistry, and English.

Subjects astronomers use are:

- math to analyze data, solve problems, and simulate astronomical events, usually done on a computer
- physics to understand what has happened and is happening in space
- chemistry to understand the make-up of celestial objects
- English to communicate with other scientists, the media, and the public

As part of their college studies, astronomy students attend lectures.

A college degree

After completing high school, most astronomy students complete a Bachelor of Science degree at college. Students usually have a main area of study in astronomy or physics.

Farther study

Astronomy students who have completed their bachelor's degree can do more study, called graduate study. Graduate students take advanced courses in astronomy and astrophysics, and do research in specific areas of astronomy. Graduate studies can take many years to complete.

After their final year of college, most students begin working as professional astronomers.

At work

Most astronomy students try to gain work experience in their field while they are studying at college. Once their college studies are finished, astronomers often take jobs with colleges, observatories, government agencies, such as NASA, planetariums, science museums, and schools. A few astronomers work in private industries, such as **aerospace** and computing.

On-the-job training

It is part of an astronomer's job to attend seminars and conferences, read scientific papers and books, and learn about new scientific equipment. It is important for astronomers to keep up to date with what is happening in their field.

Astronomers are always learning!

Some astronomers work in planetariums.

Tools and instruments

Astronomers use many different tools and instruments to do their work. They use tools and instruments in the office, in the observatory, in the laboratory, and out in space.

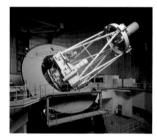

Optical telescope

Optical telescopes

Optical telescopes make distant and faint objects looker bigger and brighter. Mirrors or lenses inside optical telescopes collect and focus light to make images. Observatories containing large optical telescopes are often built on high mountains. This lifts the telescopes above some of the Earth's unsettled atmosphere, which means images are clearer.

Radio telescope

Radio telescopes

Radio telescopes collect and focus **radio waves** from objects in space. The radio waves provide information about a space object, such as its location or how fast it is moving. The part of a radio telescope that collects the radio waves is called the dish. Radio telescopes can provide information about space objects that cannot be seen with optical telescopes.

Hubble Space Telescope

Space telescopes

Space telescopes are launched into space, and orbit the Earth. Space telescopes are outside the Earth's atmosphere, which can block or distort images, so they "see" far better than ground-based telescopes.

Space probe

Probes

Probes are unoccupied spacecraft that travel to and around celestial objects, taking images and gathering data. Probes are controlled from Earth. Probes have observed eight of the nine planets in our solar system, and landed on some of them.

Rovers

An astronaut with a rover

Rovers are small robotic vehicles. A rover was used in Antarctica to search for **meteorites**. Rovers have also been used on the moon and Mars to collect and analyze samples, take photographs, and conduct experiments.

Computers

Computer

Computers are used to receive and analyze data. They are also used to develop and test theories, to control telescopes, and to simulate events in space. Astronomers also use computers to write up reports and articles, look up information on the Internet, and to send e-mails.

Spectrographs

Spectograph

Spectrographs are instruments that split radiation from a celestial object into **wavelengths**. Astronomers study the wavelengths to find out about the chemical make-up of the object they are viewing.

Star charts and atlases

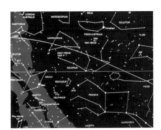

Astronomical star chart

Star charts are maps of the night sky. There are different star charts for the northern and southern hemispheres, and for different seasons. Astronomers can gain access to star charts on their computers or use printed star charts, which are sometimes bound together in a star atlas.

Cameras

Special cameras are often attached to telescopes and space probes to take images of celestial objects. Most images today are stored as computer data.

Microscopes

Microscope

Astronomers look at rock samples from space through powerful microscopes. A microscope magnifies an object or a piece of an object so that it is easier to see. Rock samples were collected when astronauts landed on the moon in 1969. Meteorites are also studied.

The Hubble Space Telescope

April 24, 1990

SHUTTLE TAKES TELESCOPE INTO ORBIT

The space shuttle *Discovery* blasted off from the Kennedy Space Center in Florida this morning with the world's largest orbiting telescope on board. The Hubble Space Telescope (HST), named after American astronomer Edwin Hubble, will be **deployed** in orbit around the Earth tomorrow.

The HST is 43.5 feet (13.2 m) long, weighs about 24,250 pounds (11,000 kg), and its main mirror is 7.9 feet (2.4 m) in diameter. Special cameras and other instruments on board the HST will enable it to take images of objects 14 billion **light-years** away. Unlike ground-based telescopes, images taken by the HST will not be blocked or changed by the Earth's atmosphere, and images can be taken 24 hours a day.

The HST will orbit approximately 375 miles (600 km) above the Earth. It is the first spacecraft to be designed to be serviced in orbit.

The HST cost 1.5 billion dollars to build and deploy, and it is expected to operate for at least 15 years. The HST project is overseen by America's National Aeronautics and Space Administration (NASA).

In 1990, the space shuttle *Discovery* blasted off from the Kennedy Space Center in Florida with the Hubble Space Telescope on board.

HUBBLE'S FIXED

Astronauts have successfully fitted a new instrument to the Hubble Space Telescope (HST) to correct a problem with the main mirror.

The astronauts reached the HST aboard the space shuttle *Endeavour.* They used a robotic arm to catch and pull the HST into the shuttle's cargo bay. During the servicing mission, other parts of the HST were also installed and replaced.

The mission took 11 days and included five space walks.

The HST was designed to be serviced in orbit.

March 12, 2002

HUBBLE IS SERVICED IN SPACE

The latest servicing mission of the Hubble Space Telescope (HST) has been successfully completed. Seven astronauts reached the HST aboard the space shuttle *Columbia.*

The astronauts performed five space walks over the 12-day mission to install and replace instruments.

The HST is expected to operate until 2007.

Modern methods

Astronomers work in observatories, laboratories, and offices. They use the latest technology to help them study the universe.

At the observatory

An observational astronomer usually spends several nights each year working at an observatory. Observatories are often in very remote places, so an astronomer must leave his or her family and home, and travel to the observatory.

Fact Box

Astronomers can also collect data from telescopes that are far away, including telescopes in space.

The telescopes are the most important pieces of equipment at an observatory. They are always in demand, and access to the telescopes is shared between many astronomers. Each astronomer has a limited amount of time with a telescope. Astronomers need to use their time wisely, so they carefully plan their work before arriving at the observatory.

To observe a celestial object with a telescope, an astronomer enters the position, called the coordinates, of the object into the telescope's computer. The telescope moves to that position, where the object can be observed. Today, it is rare for an astronomer to actually look at an object through an optical telescope. Instead, the telescope takes an image of the object and downloads it onto a computer.

Images of celestial objects are downloaded onto a computer.

In the office

Once astronomers have their data, they analyze it. This usually takes place on a computer in the astronomer's office.

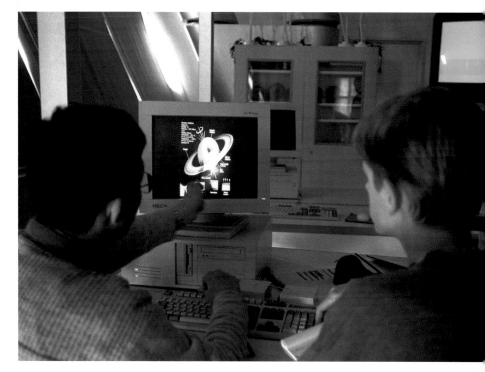

Astronomers spend a lot of time working on their computers.

Astronomers try to work out what the data means. They use the data to test their theories. They determine whether the data supports their theories. If it does not, they try to improve the theories or develop new ones. Astronomers may also decide they need to make further observations at an observatory.

The data an astronomer collects over a few days at an observatory will usually take months or longer to analyze.

Theoretical astronomers do most of their work on computers and may never use telescopes or observational equipment. Some spend all their time developing new theories. Some simulate astronomical events on computers.

Astronomers must also spend some of their time writing and reading reports and articles, answering queries, and talking with other scientists.

In the laboratory

Some astronomers work with other scientists in laboratories. They may use microscopes and other instruments to analyze rock samples from space. They want to know how old the rocks are, what they are made of, and where they came from.

Some astronomers design, build, and test new astronomical equipment.

Fact Box

Some astronomers also teach at colleges. Others work at planetariums and science museums. These astronomers play an important role in keeping the public informed about astronomy.

Working on location

Unlike most scientists, astronomers do not get close to the objects they study. Many celestial objects cannot even be seen with the naked eye. Although astronomers cannot travel to a planet, moon, star, or galaxy, they do travel to different locations on Earth to do their work.

Optical telescopes at the Mauna Kea Observatory in Hawaii

World's largest observatory

Mauna Kea, a **dormant** volcano on Hawaii, is home to the world's largest observatory.

There are 13 telescopes on Mauna Kea, and they are operated by astronomers from 11 countries. The world's largest optical telescopes, the Keck telescopes, are found there. The top of Mauna Kea is very high, more than 13,780 feet (4,200 m) above sea level. This makes it a good place for an observatory because it is above 40 percent of the Earth's atmosphere.

Astronomers go to Mauna Kea to study various celestial objects. The atmosphere above the observatory is dry and generally cloud-free, and the observatory is far from city lights. This means astronomers can get clearer images of celestial objects at Mauna Kea than almost anywhere else on Earth.

Searching for extraterrestrial intelligence

The SETI (Search for Extraterrestrial Intelligence) Institute in California uses complex astronomical equipment to search for life beyond Earth.

Astronomers who work for the institute use radio telescopes in several countries to search for signs of extraterrestrial life. They use computers to "listen" for radio signals that are being deliberately or accidentally sent to us by extraterrestrials.

There is no evidence yet that extraterrestrial life exists, but many astronomers believe it probably does. The universe is so big that there is a high chance of another planet being able to support life. If extraterrestrials do exist, we may not have heard them simply because the distance between our planets is so great.

Some people claim to have seen unidentified flying objects (UFOs) or to have been kidnapped by aliens, but there is no proof that this has happened. Writers, artists, and filmmakers have invented extraterrestrial beings, but no one really knows what a creature from another planet would look like. There are many life forms on Earth. It is likely that another planet with intelligent life would also have many different life forms.

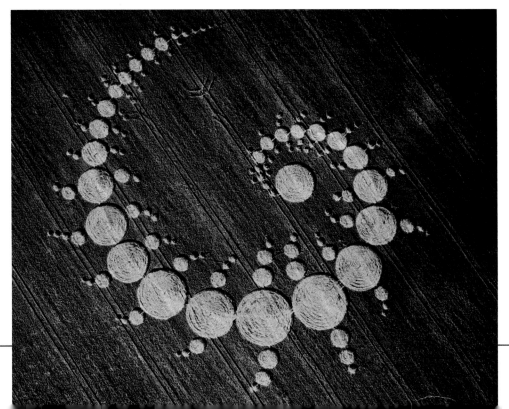

Some people think that these crop circles were created by extraterrestrials.

Yvonne Pendleton, astronomer

Dr. Yvonne Pendleton is an astrophysicist at NASA. Astrophysics is a branch of astronomy.

What does your job involve?

I travel to telescopes around the world, make observations, develop and use computer models to analyze the data, and write papers and present talks about the results. When I am at a telescope making observations, my colleagues and I begin observing around six o'clock in the evening, and we finish twelve hours later. After an observing run, we transport the data to our office computers and return to work there. The goal of my research is to understand the composition of the **organic** material found in space.

When did you first become interested in astronomy?

I was inspired by the Apollo Program. I lived in Key West, Florida, until I was 13, and I remember watching the Apollo rockets as they arched overhead from their Cape Kennedy lift-off. I would stand there looking upward, promising myself that someday I would be a part of NASA, the great agency that could take us into space.

Where did you study and what qualifications did you obtain?

I have a Bachelor of Science in Aerospace Engineering from the Georgia Institute of Technology, a Master of Science in Aeronautics and Astronautics from Stanford University, and a PhD in Astrophysics from the University of California at Santa Cruz.

Did you have a teacher who helped or inspired you in your field?

As a teenager, I spent every spare minute at the Fernbank Science Center in Atlanta, Georgia, where I was surrounded by scientists. The scientists at the center were a great source of inspiration to me.

What do you like most about your job?

Making new discoveries at the telescope is the most rewarding aspect of my job. I also like that I get the freedom to be as creative as I can be, scientifically. I choose the projects I want to investigate. The universe is a puzzle and I get to find some of the pieces.

What do you like least about your job?

I sometimes have to deal with government rules and responsibilities that take time away from my research.

Have you ever worked on an exciting project?

Right now I am most excited about the Space Infra-Red Telescope Facility (SIRTF), which is a telescope that NASA launched in August 2003. We are awaiting data from this observatory in space that will answer many questions about star formation and dust in the universe.

A test flight for the SOFIA project

What advances are likely to occur in astronomy?

There are many missions already on the way to Mars and Saturn, plus missions currently being designed to study other planets and more distant objects, and these will likely provide answers to many questions. The Stratospheric Observatory For Infra-Red Astronomy (SOFIA) is a great example of the exciting times ahead for astronomers. This unique facility will fly a telescope inside a Boeing 747 jet and it will allow observations above most of the Earth's atmosphere.

What advice would you give to young people interested in a career in astronomy?

Long hours and dedication to your studies now will put you in a good position later, so don't take the easy road. Follow your dreams and believe in yourself. Even when you think you aren't good enough for the task ahead of you, be confident. You'll surprise yourself!

The amazing universe

Welcome to Astronomer Al's website! Got a question about the amazing universe? Email it to Astronomer Al. He'll be happy to answer it.

Dear AA
How many planets are there in our solar system?
Pedro

Dear Pedro

There are nine planets in our solar system. They are Mercury, Venus, Earth, Mars, Jupiter, Saturn, Uranus, Neptune, and Pluto. They all orbit the sun. There are also many other bodies in our solar system, such as moons, **comets**, **asteroids**, and **meteoroids**.

AA

Dear AA
Why is the Earth called a rocky planet?
Zena

Dear Zena

Mercury, Venus, Earth, and Mars are called rocky planets because they have hard surfaces and are made mainly of rock. Jupiter, Saturn, Uranus, and Neptune are much larger. They are called gas giants because they are made mainly of gas. Pluto is a small planet of rock and ice that doesn't fit into either group.

AA

Hello AA
What is the sun made of? Is it really a star?
Henri

Dear Henri

The sun is a huge ball of hot gases. It is a star. It looks bigger and brighter than other stars because it is the star closest to Earth. The sun gives us light and heat. NEVER LOOK AT THE SUN DIRECTLY. YOU MIGHT DAMAGE YOUR EYES.

AA

Hi AA
Does the moon change shape?
Alanna

Hi Alanna

The moon does not change shape. The moon makes no light of its own, instead we see the sun's light reflecting off it. As the moon orbits the Earth, different parts of it are lit up at different times. This makes the moon appear to change shape.

AA

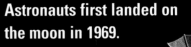

Astronauts first landed on the moon in 1969.

Dear AA
How long is a year on other planets?
Alex

Dear Alex

It takes each planet one of its years to orbit the sun. The planets closer to the sun have shorter years. One year on each planet is the following length:

Mercury = 88 Earth days
Venus = 224.7 Earth days
Earth = 365.25 Earth days
Mars = 687 Earth days
Jupiter = 11.86 Earth years

Saturn = 29.46 Earth years
Uranus = 84 Earth years
Neptune = 164.8 Earth years
Pluto = 248 Earth years

AA

Hi AA
What is the Milky Way?
Huan

Hi Huan

The Milky Way is the name of our galaxy. A galaxy is a huge group of stars, gas, and dust. Galaxies such as the Milky Way contain hundreds of billions of stars.

AA

Astronomy in the future

Astronomy is often called the oldest science because people have always been able to look at objects in the sky without needing special equipment or scientific knowledge. Modern astronomers know a lot about the universe, but there is much more to learn. One thing is certain, astronomy in the future will be very exciting.

More complex equipment

In the future, astronomers will use more complex equipment to gather more information about celestial objects.

Better telescopes will be used to "see" further into the universe, including the Next Generation Space Telescope that NASA will launch. This telescope will gather more light and take better images than the Hubble Space Telescope.

In the future, an observatory may be built on the moon.

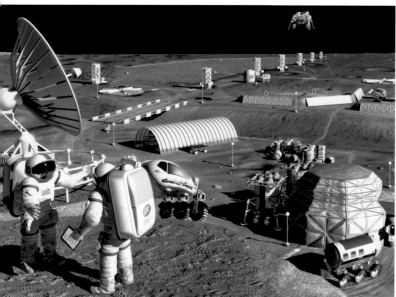

Existing observatories on Earth will be improved. An observatory may even be built on the moon, maybe even Mars!

More powerful computers will be used to receive and analyze data. They will also be used to simulate and model events in the past and future of the universe with greater accuracy.

More probes will be sent to planets in our solar system, including Pluto.

People in space

Future spacecraft will be faster and more advanced. They will probably carry people once again to the moon, and even to Mars.

Several space stations have already been launched. The International Space Station is currently in orbit. At the moment, it functions as a laboratory, and is just for working astronauts. One day space stations may act as hotels for people wanting to take a vacation in space.

Beyond our solar system

Extrasolar planets are planets in other solar systems. An extrasolar planet orbits its sun, just as the Earth orbits our sun. In the distant future, probes may be able to visit and even land on extrasolar planets. We may even find life on extrasolar planets!

The International Space Station is now in orbit.

As we continue to search for extraterrestrial life, with better equipment and greater knowledge, contact may be made.

Astronomers still have many questions about the universe. How did it begin? How big is it? What is it made of? What will happen to it in the future? Perhaps in the future, astronomers will find some of the answers.

Get involved in astronomy

You can get involved in astronomy by studying the night sky. You can see some objects with your eyes, but it is better to use binoculars or a telescope. Here are some fun activities you might like to try.

Draw the moon

You will need:

- warm clothes
- binoculars or a telescope
- large sketchpad
- pencil

What to do:

1 On a dry, clear night, when the moon is almost full, put on warm clothes.
2 Go outside and look up at the moon with your binoculars or telescope.
3 Draw the outline of the moon on your sketchpad. Make it large so you can add details.
4 Find seas (these are called seas, but are really plains of solidified **lava**) on the moon. Draw them on your sketchpad.
5 Find craters on the moon and draw them on your sketchpad.
6 Find mountains on the moon and draw them on your sketchpad.
7 Compare your drawing with these pictures of the moon.

This is the moon as it looks from the northern hemisphere.

This is the moon as it looks from the southern hemisphere.

The expanding universe

Astronomers have discovered that the universe is expanding. This activity will show you what that means.

You will need:

- balloon
- rubber band or a twist-tie
- small dot stickers

What to do:

1 Partly blow up the balloon. The rubber surface represents the universe.
2 Tie the balloon off with the rubber band or twist-tie so that no air escapes.
3 Place stickers over the balloon. The stickers represent galaxies.

4 Remove the rubber band or twist-tie.
5 Blow up the balloon some more. Can you see how the stickers move apart? That is what happens to galaxies as the universe expands. The space between the galaxies gets bigger. The galaxies themselves do not expand because they are held together by gravity.

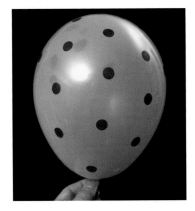

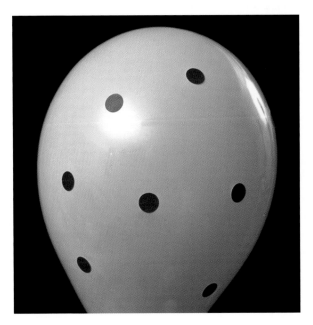

More to do

Get your whole class involved in astronomy!

- Put up star charts around your classroom.

- Ask your teacher to arrange a class trip to a planetarium.

- Study a different planet each week.

- Ask an astronomer to give a talk to your class.

Check it out!

Astronomy is an exciting science. You can learn more about astronomy, and the jobs of astronomers, by checking out some of these places and Web sites.

The night sky

Study the night sky. You can see many interesting features with the naked eye, and even more with binoculars or a telescope. Dress warmly, use a star chart to find stars, a compass to find north, and a watch to note the time of your observations. Write down any interesting facts in a notebook, and make sketches. Carry a torch, but cover it with red cellophane. Red light will not spoil your night vision.

Planetariums offer exciting astronomy shows.

Astronomy clubs and planetariums

Join an astronomy club. Some clubs organize trips to observatories and areas where you can observe the night sky away from city lights. Some even show you how to build a telescope.

A planetarium or science museum is a great place to learn about astronomy. At most planetariums, you can watch exciting shows about celestial objects.

Web sites

NASA Kids   http://kids.msfc.nasa.gov
StarChild   http://starchild.gsfc.nasa.gov/docs/StarChild/StarChild.html
American Astronomical Society   http://www.aas.org
The SETI Institute   http://www.seti.org
The Nine Planets   http://www.seds.org/nineplanets/nineplanets/nineplanets.html

Glossary

abjure formally swear that you have given up certain ideas and beliefs

aerospace spacecraft technology

asteroids lumps of rock that orbit the sun, mostly found between Mars and Jupiter

black holes massive objects in space which are so dense that not even light can escape their gravitational pull

celestial in the sky or heavens

comets bodies of ice and dust that orbit the sun

deployed prepared for use

dormant inactive, not erupting

heresy having opinions or beliefs that are different to the teachings and beliefs of the Church

lava hot liquid rock

light-years measurements of distance in space. One light-year is the distance light travels in a year (5.86 trillion miles or 9.46 trillion km)

lunar eclipse an event when the Earth passes between the moon and sun, blocking out the sun's light on the moon

matter the substance or substances of which objects are made

meteorites meteoroids that have fallen to the Earth

meteoroids particles of dust or rock in space

microwave radiation a type of energy that we cannot see, because it has wavelengths that are longer than visible light

organic made up of a substance called carbon, usually combined with other substances such as hydrogen and nitrogen

phases how a moon or planet looks from the Earth at different times depending on how much of the surface we see is lit by the sun's light

radio waves energy that we cannot see and that has very long wavelengths

simulate to model or reproduce an event, object, or situation

sunspots dark patches that sometimes appear on the surface of the sun

theories statements that have not yet been proved, but can be tested

wavelengths energies of different lengths

Index

Pages 10–11 Who am I? answer:
Galileo Galilei